change
for the better

business change
for decision makers

FORMAT
PUBLISHING

Published by
Format Publishing Limited
9-10 Redwell Street
Norwich
Norfolk NR2 4SN
United Kingdom

www.formatpublishing.co.uk

First published 2003
ISBN 1903091284

British Library Cataloguing in Publication data
A CIP record for this book is available from the
British Library

This publication *Change for the better: business
change for decision makers* is based upon source
material which is either Crown copyright and/or Crown
copyright with value added product status. Such
material has been reused and refocused under licence
from and with the kind permission of the Controller of
HMSO and the Office of Government Commerce.

Cover illustration: *Men jumping hurdles* by SIS
Ltd/Bruno Budrovic
Other illustrations by Digital Vision

Printed in the UK by Norwich Colour Print on paper
derived from replenishable forests maintained with
'two-for-one' planting

contents

1

introduction

- Why manage change?
- How this book can help
- Factors for success

Change is a constant in today's business world, and the ability to manage it effectively is a vital management skill. Changing the business for the better is the goal of every manager and decision maker. Whatever the reason – new competition, changing markets, new technologies, or just the desire to improve – there is always scope for change.

Why manage change?

No business stands still. In fact, in today's business environment, change has become a constant. Changes in the business environment, new customer demands, advances in technology, and changing expectations of staff are just a few of the pressures that force continual change on every business.

Poorly managed change can be catastrophic for the business. A clear idea of what constitutes success, realism about the business's capability to change, and detailed plans for how the change will be achieved are all vital; none of them will happen by accident. Without them, there is a very real danger that new structures or ways of working will be created that do not deliver any real benefits – or deliver the wrong kinds of benefit, drawing the business away from realising its key aims. Even worse, the change effort may actually waste resources, achieve little, and force you to start over again. The wider the scope of the proposed change, the greater the potential for problems.

The worst case scenario is that the change becomes an unfocused, indefinite period of upheaval that is embarked on without direction, continued without focus or monitoring, and ended when those involved are unable to continue.

How this book can help

All businesses are different, as are the changes they need to make. There is no perfect prescription that will work in all situations.

Business change can be a complex process, and one that touches many areas of management. But if the right questions are asked at the right time, and important issues faced with realism and pragmatism, the chances of successful change are much improved.

change for the better

what distinguishes the successes from the failures?

This guide will give you an overview of the steps you need to take, and the questions you need to ask at each stage, to manage change successfully. Following the advice in the following pages will give you a much clearer idea of what you need to do and how you can go about achieving it.

Factors for success

Everyone has lived through attempts to introduce changes in their business, some more successful than others. Sometimes, far-reaching changes are implemented with relative ease. Other apparently minor changes result in unintended consequences and disruption beyond all expectations. What distinguishes the successes from the failures?

- **clear aims:** those planning and leading the change have a clear understanding of its purpose

- **management commitment:** senior management fully understand the change, agree with the reasons for it, and are committed to its success

- **recognising complexity:** those in charge of the change fully understand the interdependencies involved

- **change owner:** a single figure has been nominated as the head of the change effort, in whom responsibility rests and to whom questions and problems are ultimately referred

- **the right team:** those involved have the right skills, abilities and experience to manage all the issues – practical and cultural – that will arise

- **communication and involvement:** everyone who will be affected by the change knows their role, what the change will mean for them, and how the business will be different after the change

- **staff development and support:** those who have to implement the change or who will be at the cutting edge of any new business processes are fully trained and supported in new areas

- **making it stick:** new ways of working must be adopted and seen to be an improvement; the change must be managed so that reverting to old methods does not come to seem attractive, or even inevitable.

change for the better

2

origins

this chapter outlines the change process, which is covered in the following chapters, and looks at the reasons and drivers for change and the importance of deciding where you want change to take you.

The change process

Every change process is different, but there are certain key questions that have to be asked and answered as change unfolds. They are shown in the diagram and expanded in the following chapters.

Starting point

Why change?

Where do you want to be?

Have the benefits been realised?

Where are you now?

The change process

How will you take people with you?

What needs to change?

What approach will you take?

Are you ready for change?

change for the better

The origin of change lies in the perception that something is wrong, or could be improved, or a new opportunity has arisen. This answers the question 'why change?' It is important to answer this question, so that you can gauge whether change has been successful later.

Taking stock (chapter 3) means asking three questions: 'where are we now?', 'where do we want to be?', 'what needs to change?' and 'how do we get there?' Answering these questions may not be as simple as it sounds – it could involve challenging received ideas about the business, what it should be doing, and what really needs to change to make that a reality.

Readiness (chapter 4) is a huge issue. It is one thing to set out a route map for change, quite another to take people with you on the journey. You need to consider carefully the attitudes, beliefs and motives of everyone involved. You also need to think about the risks involved in change, and whether you are ready to take them on.

The way in which change will be approached (chapter 5) must be carefully considered, and it is vital to think through the human side of change as well as the practical aspects (chapters 6 and 7). Finally, it is important to review the change (chapter 8) to see whether the benefits that were hoped for really came about.

After a major change effort, everyone will probably be hoping for a period of stability. But periods of 'steady state' are unlikely to last long. New factors in the business environment, or even issues raised when reviewing a change process, can point the way forward to the need or opportunity for further changes.

The stages of the change process will involve iteration and backtracking, negotiation and experimentation. Some may have to be done out of sequence. But the key questions remain the same.

origins

Why change?

You need to be clear on why the business needs to change, since the areas in which you should concentrate your efforts will depend on what, in the broadest sense, is driving change. Even if the reason for change seems obvious, it is worth considering it from first principles. There may be other reasons for changing that are also important, or those that are perceived as crucial may in fact be less so.

Drivers for change and stability

One way to analyse the reason for change is to consider it as the result of one or more drivers for change – the factors that push the business towards change. It is important to understand all the drivers pushing the business toward change. It will help to focus your thoughts on where effort should be concentrated. Drivers for change might include:

- the need to provide better services for customers
- the need to improve performance
- the need to save costs or reduce overheads
- market pressure from competitors
- the need for the business's culture to reflect societal changes
- pressures to maintain morale and cohesion, to motivate and develop staff, and treat them fairly; pressures for empowerment of staff
- the need for better support for the business's activities (premises, infrastructure or information management systems).

There may also be drivers that resist change, driving the business to stand still – these are known as drivers for stability. They are often cultural rather than concrete in nature, and might include:

- adherence to company tradition, 'the way we do things here'
- unwillingness to acknowledge problems
- fear of the unknown
- concern over the risks of changing
- existing management structures
- informal power structures or 'pecking orders'
- failing to consult or inform those affected by the change.

Every business has a strong tendency to remain as it is. Infrastructure is costly to change; hierarchies and power structures evolve slowly

change for the better

(if at all); people tend not to change their ways of working spontaneously, or may resist such change if it is imposed upon them.

Because of their cultural, unofficial nature, drivers for stability can be difficult to define, change, or even perceive from within the business. But their influence must be taken into account when planning a change. People outside the business, or who have joined recently, may be best placed to analyse them. People who have been inside it for a long time may find them harder to discern; bear in mind that such people may include the senior management whose approval and commitment will be vital to the change.

Gaining commitment to the change will be simpler if a direct linkage can be made between the driver(s) and the objectives of the change, for example: 'changes in customer expectations mean that we must offer services online to retain a share of our target market'.

If due attention is not paid to the underlying drivers of change, no amount of management effort or investment will make the change a success.

every business has a strong tendency to remain as it is

Force field analysis

Force field analysis is a useful technique to identify the forces acting on the business. It helps to identify where effort will be required in assisting the change and overcoming resistance to it.

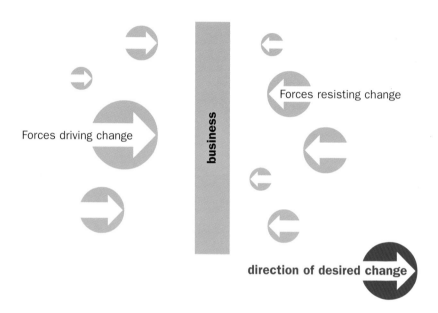

The diagram shows a business in a state of dynamic tension. There are forces at work, pushing in different directions, that have settled into a state of equilibrium and cancel each other out. If one or more driving forces in the situation can be strengthened, or one or more restraining forces weakened, then the situation will be shifted in the direction of the desired change.

You need to make some estimate of the 'strength' of each force. Once this is done, attention should be focused on the strongest forces, since addressing one or two of those could make all the difference in effecting the desired change.

It is important to describe the forces in terms that enable the necessary action to be identified; you need to be able to do something about strengthening or weakening the force as described. For example, if there is resistance to the introduction of an IT system because a

change for the better

define a goal
for the change

previous attempt failed, the restraining force could be 'concern about the chances of success'. Attention can then be focused on weakening that force, for example by finding ways to address concerns and showing that lessons have been learned.

Where do you want to be?

It is essential to define a goal for the change – the outcome that you are hoping to bring about through change.

Goals should be specific and universally understood. If you are going to establish a new operation, decide what 'established' means. If the goal is savings or revenue, decide how much is enough. If you want to streamline an operation, decide on its ideal new form. Goals that are relative or hard to measure will not be helpful to you when reviewing the change process later on. They will give you a direction, but not a destination.

Make the goal challenging enough to arouse people's interest and enthusiasm – to create a sense of something new to be aimed for. If you already have a stated goal or goals, try to devise a new form of words even though your aim may not have changed a great deal.

Offset a sense of realism against the need for a challenge. If the desired goal could never be achieved with the resources you have (or will have) available, you are bound to fail. Keep it realistic as well as challenging. It may be helpful to think of a distillation of the sentiments people at all levels often have about the kind of business you could be, 'if only…'.

The change goal should help to focus your thoughts on the change process. This is because it is immutable – unlike your expectations of the change process, which are likely to change as you progress into the stages of taking stock and planning. The change goal can form the yardstick against which the results of the change process are measured. Throughout the change process and particularly during the final stages of review, when you look back on the process and gauge the benefits, it will serve as a useful reminder of the core purpose of the change and a means of assessing its success.

3

taking stock

his chapter covers taking stock of where the business is and deciding on the scope of change: answering the questions 'where are you now?' and 'what needs to change?'

Where are you now?

Before you decide what will change, you must understand where you are starting from. On the simplest level, if you 'subtract' where you are now from where you want to be, you will be left with what needs to change to get you there.

If extensive change programmes are in prospect, it may be helpful to produce a report on the current status of the business, or commission an unbiased survey from management consultants or other impartial sources. Such a report could help to dispel 'myths' and assumptions about the business – both positive and negative – that might prejudice the change planning process.

The baseline and the 'do nothing' option

The baseline is the starting point for change. It expresses the state of the business at present; a 'snapshot' that encompasses procedures, structures and performance but makes no assumptions about the future. It is useful for gauging the success of change in a 'before and after' sense – working out whether changes have resulted in real improvements in comparison with what went before.

When considering change, and assuming that the change is not being forced upon you, there is always the option to do nothing or simply continue operating as at present – the baseline option. Often appealing to businesses facing an uncertain future, the baseline option seems to offer a risk-free short- or medium-term strategy. It is particularly compelling for businesses that have already undergone major change, for whom plunging into further investment might seem ill advised.

However, there are risks associated with doing nothing. Be realistic about the prospects for improvement if nothing changes; does past performance suggest you will trade your way out of trouble?
The status quo may not be as cheap to maintain as you think. You may be incurring a staff-time overhead as people work around ill-defined procedures or spend too much time 'fire-fighting'. Staff in different

change for the better

is doing nothing an option?

departments may be solving the same problems independently because there is no coherent strategy for sharing knowledge.

You will also need to be aware of what might be around the corner if you do not change. For example, if your existing IT systems come to the end of their economic life, staying at the baseline will imply replacing them with something that replicates the same functionality, possibly at significant cost. If work volumes increase, you may not have sufficient capacity. In situations like these, a 'do nothing' strategy may end up forcing the business into a position of unplanned or hasty change when a crisis is reached – often handled by those 'at the sharp end' rather than those with an overview of what the business needs.

You must consider carefully the real costs and implications of 'doing nothing' if you propose it as an option. However, it may be that after careful consideration it does emerge as the best option; for example if change is simply too risky or costly for your business at the present time. If so, revisit your situation later to take stock once again.

What kind of change?

Some changes are anticipated. The need for them can be foreseen, and they are done voluntarily to reach planned objectives. Planned changes include:

- **improving efficiency:** doing what you do more quickly, or doing more of it in the same time

- **improving effectiveness:** doing what you do better, preferably without a trade-off in terms of cost or time

- **improving economy:** spending less money for the same results

- **moving into new areas of business:** offering new services, or the same services in a new way

- **withdrawing** from existing areas of business

- **restructuring** following the merging or separating of two businesses, or the acquisition of one business by another.

Other changes are unforeseen and obligatory. Examples include:

- **correcting a problem** that has been neglected, ignored or not fully appreciated until now

- responding to **adverse business conditions** – new competition, for example

- utilising a **new technology** that cannot be ignored

- responding to the needs of an important or major **new customer** who is ready to work with you.

Another unplanned change (which this guide should help you avoid) is recovering from a change effort that has failed: undoing what has been changed and restoring the business to its previous state. The need for rapid action is often a hallmark of unplanned change; planned changes afford the luxury of taking longer over the process.

The nature of the change you are facing affects your approach. It would not be helpful to adopt a cautious, step-by-step approach if the business is losing money every day – even if you find a perfect solution, it might come too late. Conversely, if the business is healthy it would be foolish to move into radically new areas of business without careful planning and consideration of all the risks.

change for the better

it is better to cross a river successfully than sink without trace in an ocean

The boundaries of change

Before considering what will change, how, and who will be affected, it is important to define the boundaries of the change. Businesses are complex systems of people, structures, technology, culture, processes and management, operating in an environment that is itself complex and constantly changing. A change in any one of these elements can have repercussions elsewhere, and the unintended consequences of even minor changes can, in the worst case, destabilise the whole change effort. It is therefore vital to define the boundaries of what will change, as far as is possible.

A relatively simple, bounded situation where change can be achieved without repercussions can be described as a 'difficulty'. A situation with large and complex sets of interacting problems can be described as a 'mess'. Messes are essentially unbounded – it is not easy to say exactly where to 'draw the line' and exclude certain factors from consideration.

Difficulties	Messes
Essentially bounded in scope	Essentially unbounded in scope
Limited number of people involved; easy to identify them	Not easy to identify all the people involved
Objectives clear and well understood	Objectives unclear; no agreement on objectives
Priorities clear	Uncertainty over priorities
What needs to be changed is clear	Disagreement over what the problem is
Solutions are easily identified	Not clear what would constitute a 'solution'
All relevant information is known or accessible	Not clear what information is relevant; or information is unreliable or hard to find
Timescale is known	More time required, or timescale hard to define
People involved hold the same views and values	Values differ among those involved

change for the better

The differences between difficulties and messes are summarised in the table opposite. You may find that you recognise characteristics of 'messy' changes you have lived through or observed.

It is important to know whether you are facing a difficulty or a mess. If you are faced with a mess, and assume that it is only a difficulty, your chances of success will be reduced. A mismanaged change could turn a difficulty into a mess.

Rather than embarking on a 'mess' – an unbounded, unfocused change effort where neither the starting point nor the objectives are clear – try to ensure that all problems are foreseeable and that they can be considered as 'difficulties'.

If the change seems too large or unmanageable, consider breaking it down into more easily achievable modules, or approaching the end result by increments (see chapter 5). It is better to cross a river successfully than sink without trace in an ocean.

The boundaries of change may also extend beyond your business, involving your customers or suppliers. Suppliers, in particular, may have a major stake if you plan to change the way you work – they must be able to keep up with what you are planning.

What needs to change?

Having established where the business stands and the kind of change that is in prospect, you need to scope the change: to ask, at a general level, 'what do you want to change?'

Defining the scope of the change does not mean specifying it in detail. There will still be some uncertainty about what exactly will be changing, and how change will take place. For far-reaching changes, it may not even be possible to reach complete agreement on objectives. None of this means you should abandon the attempt to define the scope of change with as much accuracy as you can.

Scoping should give a clearer view of the implications of the proposed change – an understanding of the change's anticipated effects on the business and its environment.

Change may affect the following areas of the business:

- **strategy:** how the proposed change supports business strategy, and how strategy might have to be altered to reflect the outcome of the change

in the real world,
there will be
conflicting priorities
and limited resources

- **structure:** the physical and organisational structure of the business, its functions and processes and their relationships, the products it makes and the services it delivers

- **management:** management structures and processes, sources of power and influence, responsibilities, reporting arrangements, performance management, information flows

- **people:** the roles and responsibilities of individuals and workgroups, requirements for skills, training and job flexibility, and cultural impact – changes in values, behaviours and attitudes

- **resources:** the funds and assets that are used by the business in its work

- **technology:** the need for new or different IT, facilities for communication and information management, and the sourcing and management of IT facilities.

Prioritisation

In a perfect world, there would be enough time and money to change whatever was necessary. In the real world, there will be conflicting priorities and limited resources. There may be more than one change initiative planned, and only finite resources available. You may need to decide which changes should go ahead now, and which can wait. This is known as prioritisation. Its aim is to create a list of possible initiatives in descending order of importance, giving an indication of their relative priority. (New business needs and conflicting resource demands could change this list later.)

Prioritisation puts investment decisions on a rational footing rather than an emotional one. It means that you go ahead with those changes that will deliver the most value first, making the best possible use of scarce resources and reducing the risk of missing business opportunities.

While particular options may offer 'quick wins' (see chapter 5) or highly desirable short-term benefits, it is important that you put the needs of the business and your customers first – and that you are seen to be doing so.

Other initiatives currently in progress could affect the change, so an important part of prioritisation is to ensure that these have been taken into account. There could be implications for your change if finite resources in vital components of your business are already committed elsewhere (or soon will be). IT departments, for example, might already be in the process of implementing changes for another department, or troubleshooting in the aftermath of a change. Your contingency plans for such resource issues might include scaling down or delaying part of the planned change.

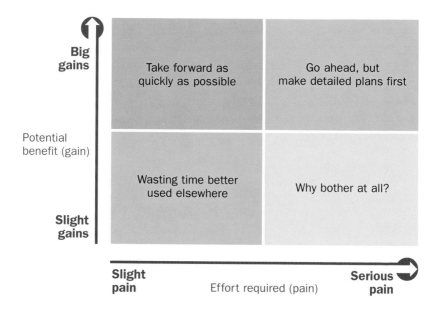

A simple technique for assessing priority is the pain/gain matrix, shown above. Each option can be assessed against two factors:

- the benefit it will realise
- the effort required to make it happen.

Options that fall near the bottom right of the matrix are complex or difficult to achieve and fail to deliver much benefit, prompting questions about whether they are worth pursuing at all. At the opposite corner, options that deliver significant benefit and are easy to take forward should be moved forward as quickly as possible.

Options in the bottom left of the matrix are simple to effect but have low impact. It may be that resources are better directed to other options, at least in the short term. Changes in the top right of the matrix are probably worthwhile, but their complexity means that careful planning will be required.

change for the better

4

are you ready for change?

being ready for change is half the battle. Readiness is not just about making detailed, practical plans for change; it is also about recognising the complexity of what is coming, particularly in its human aspects.

Unitary and pluralist

You have to understand the nature of the business you are changing. A useful distinction is that between 'unitary' and 'pluralist' organisations.

In a 'unitary' organisation, all members hold a common view of objectives, and are committed to working together in support of those objectives. Authority is vested in those appointed to positions of power, and conflict is seen as dysfunctional. Decisions are taken on a purely rational basis.

In a 'pluralist' organisation, 'politics' and personalities have much more influence. There may be many sources of power other than the recognised authority figures – for example, the 'expert power' exercised by those with particular skills or knowledge. Conflict is seen as inevitable and something to be managed, possibly leading to beneficial outcomes. Decisions are taken as a result of processes of negotiation, compromise and accommodation.

When planning your change, you will need to guard against making too many 'unitary' assumptions about the culture of your business, and ensure that you have taken account of all the 'pluralist' realities with which you will have to contend – conflicts of interest, multiple power sources, and so on.

A 'unitary' approach to change will assume that change can be imposed by legitimate authority, and will be accepted by the organisation as a necessary objective. Management will assume that all members of the organisation will be committed to the change by virtue of their support for the power structure and their willingness to maintain unity. Taking this kind of approach in an organisation that is really a 'pluralist' one is unlikely to be effective.

The processes of decision-making will also influence the approach to change. Change efforts tend to be more successful in those organisations in which there is a high degree of participation by members of staff in decision-making – one of the hallmarks of the 'pluralist' organisation.

change for the better

Stakeholders

A stakeholder is anyone who will be affected by the change.

In any change situation there will be those who support the change and those who oppose it. There will be those who gain from it and those who lose – and those who are convinced they will lose despite all evidence to the contrary. There will be those who anticipate an opportunity and those who see only a threat. And of course there will be those who are indifferent to the change; this may turn out to be helpful or unhelpful, depending on the influence they have. Stakeholders' positions are also likely to be linked to the amount of change they themselves will have to make.

Examples of stakeholders you will probably need to consider are:

- people whose work will be affected
- customers
- suppliers
- shareholders, the board of directors, the chief executive, steering committees and so on
- those who control the assignment of resources, including external agencies (such as banks)
- those who control the movement, recruitment or training of staff.

who will be affected?

A vital component of the change process is identifying stakeholders and taking account of their views on the change. The aim is to bring everyone who has a stake in the change on board and to make them feel not only that they are part of the change, but that they will benefit from it as well. Their initial positions may be rational and justifiable, or emotional and unfounded, but they must all be taken into account. In some cases they have the power to insist that the change takes place, to veto it, or to determine the desired outcome.

Not all stakeholders are equally important; they should be considered in terms of the amount of influence they can bring to bear, and their sympathy with the aims and objectives of the change. Creating a stakeholder map, illustrating the influences, interests and relationships of stakeholders regarding the change and each other, may help to clarify your thoughts on how to approach the task of generating enthusiasm and commitment for change.

Complexity and dependencies

Complexity is a key issue. A change in one area of the business may have a knock-on effect elsewhere. There may be other businesses – suppliers or customers – with a stake in the proposed change. Recognising and managing these links and interdependencies will be vital in a successful change.

For example, a change programme aimed at introducing IT facilities to improve administrative efficiency may conflict with an existing programme of staff redeployment, or cut across well-established arrangements for assigning tasks. Similarly, the introduction of new customer-oriented services may create problems for human resource functions, but generate opportunities for reduced overheads. Issues such as these are complex both in their scope (affecting different areas of the business) and in their dimensions, which could be technical, practical, political and (last but not least) human.

change for the better

Uncertainty and different perspectives

In an ideal world, change would be based on a clear understanding of the desired outcomes and the actions required to achieve them, coupled with a stable environment in which to work towards them. However, in many situations, and particularly those involving anything other than the simplest of changes, you will have to work in an uncertain world. Almost certainly, there will be different perspectives on the change and its objectives among stakeholders.

Uncertainty about change has two dimensions. The first dimension is lack of agreement over 'ends', or what you are trying to achieve; for example, the views of management and staff on the objectives for the introduction of new IT-based facilities might vary. While some differences in outlook are quite natural, particularly for wide-ranging change, you must make a distinction between this situation, where a consensus to take action may be enough to begin change, and a genuine confusion or disagreement over your aims. If the desired outcome is unclear, it will be impossible to tell whether the change has been successful.

concentrate on areas
of agreement to find
a way forward

The second dimension is disagreement over 'means', or how the objective is to be achieved; for example, all concerned agree that overheads must be reduced, but the areas to be targeted for savings have yet to be agreed. This kind of uncertainty is to be expected, and indeed it is better that the ways to achieve change are over-analysed rather than a course of action being chosen by default, in haste, or for short-term convenience. The change owner will need to involve all stakeholders in discussions over how change will be achieved, and concentrate on areas of agreement to find a way forward.

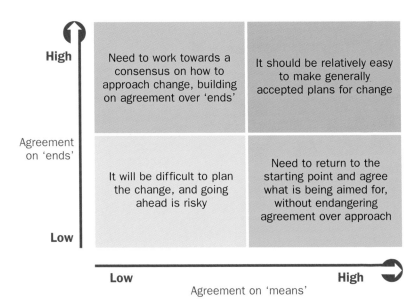

The two dimensions of uncertainty are shown on the diagram. The situation in the top right-hand quadrant – good agreement on objectives, and reasonable certainty about how to achieve them – suggests that the change effort will be well defined and relatively easy to plan. For more complex changes, the situation is more likely to be that in the bottom left-hand quadrant. Here, the change effort will have to confront varying expectations and deal with uncertainties. Techniques for moving from the low/low quadrant to the high/high quadrant include reducing risk by taking more cautious approaches to change (see the next chapter), and pilot programmes.

External stakeholders such as customers and key suppliers may also have influential views on the change. If the aim of the change is to

change for the better

improve services to customers, their perspective (known or assumed) on what you are changing must be kept in mind throughout the change. Over time, it is all too easy to allow the convenience of the business to supplant the needs of the customer as the objective of change, with disastrous long-term results.

Is the culture ready?

Never underestimate the importance of taking people with you in change. People may not feel that their interests are best served by the change, and may even see reason to resist or obstruct the change. Resistance or lack of understanding about change often has its roots in the culture of a business.

Culture can be summed up as 'the way we do things around here'. Businesses define and order themselves 'top-down' by means of hierarchies, job descriptions, lines of command, business strategies and other formal devices. But as anyone who has worked for a living knows, this is only half the story. On the other side of the coin are the accepted ideas, myths, unwritten rules, power struggles, personality clashes, rivalries, pecking orders, rumours and history that make up the business's culture.

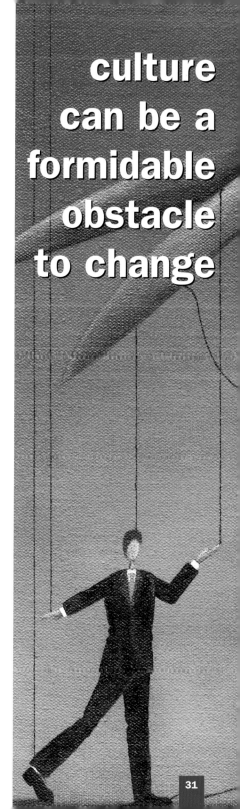

culture can be a formidable obstacle to change

An entrenched culture can persist for many years, through thick and thin, in spite of personnel changes, even against the will of senior management. Clearly, culture can be a formidable obstacle to change, and should not be underestimated. Be aware also that a highly radical change may simply be too far-reaching for the culture to absorb, even though the drivers for change and your vision for the future make it clear that it is necessary. If so, consider whether a series of modular or incremental changes might be more appropriate (see chapter 5).

For many changes, the culture beyond the business itself may be equally important; for example the attitudes of your clients or customers may need to be changed if you are planning to provide a radically new service for them.

What went before

Take account of recent change efforts and their results, particularly those that failed, succeeded only partially, or damaged morale. They are gone and beyond your control, but they have a strong bearing on how much change the business's culture can stand. If you are new to the business, spend some time talking to those who were affected by the change, to gain the benefit of their hindsight.

If staff feel that recent changes were not successful, they may be resistant to further changes. Similar feelings may be engendered by the perception that change was handed down from 'on high' rather than based on grass-roots requirements. In such cases, techniques for communication, training and overcoming resistance (see chapter 6) will be vital to success.

It may also be simply too soon for a far-reaching change; if a radical change has recently been implemented, whatever its perceived or actual success, it may be too soon to attempt further change on such a scale. Consider a more gradual approach to 'soften the blow'.

change for the better

5

making it happen

- Transformational change
- Incremental and modular change
- Quick wins
- Transition
- Unfreezing and refreezing

how will you approach the change? One of the first questions to answer is how quick the change needs to be (or can be). Taking things slowly can improve your chances of success. This chapter looks at three ways to approach change and what happens before and after it.

Transformational change

In transformational change (also known as 'big-bang' or 'discontinuous' change) the entire change is planned and implemented in one go. Even if the change involves many related projects, or touches on difference areas of the business, the aim is to achieve everything together, in as short a time as possible.

Transformational change carries a high degree of risk. A complex change will demand a great deal of effort and management commitment. If you decide that a 'short, sharp shock' is the best way to change, it follows that the shock should be as short as possible; this also implies full-time management of the change while it is in progress. You must realistically assess whether your business can afford such commitment to the change and maintain its normal business processes – or you may end up simply prolonging the confusion and upheaval.

Transformational change is likely to work best when the change is clearly bounded, and there is strong agreement on objectives and how the change should be made. Having considered this in chapter 4, you can now decide whether this is right for you.

There are times when the 'big-bang' approach is the only way. Perhaps the change has to coincide with other developments, or comply with new legislative requirements, or it may be impossible to continue with old processes for some reason.

Another perspective on rapid change is that it can be a way of overcoming cultural resistance, by minimising the period during which dissent can arise. However, this is a high-risk tactic, and runs counter to the principles of communication and involvement that are the hallmarks of successful changes. Try the 'softer' approaches covered in chapter 6 first.

Incremental and modular change

An incremental change is achieved gradually, through an evolutionary process. The change is made step by step; after each step you can assess the results and determine whether the overall objective is still appropriate. This approach carries less risk of failure than big-bang change, although there is a risk of change taking so long that it is overtaken by events and new drivers for change emerge.

In a situation where external pressures are continually shifting, objectives are changing or unclear, and the impact of the changes is difficult to predict, the incremental approach helps you to maintain control over the change process.

The incremental approach does not rule out radical change. A distant goal can still be approached incrementally. It may even be useful to be able to refine your expectations, or those of stakeholders, as events unfold. Incremental change involves techniques such as phased build-up of new functions, facilities or services, or the gradual roll-out of new systems across departments or geographical regions. Each step must leave the business in a state of equilibrium, from which it can move forward to the next step.

In modular change the change is broken down into discrete, more easily achievable 'packages', each of which offers some benefit, even when the others are not yet complete. As opposed to incremental change, which offers the full change benefit to part of the business first, then expands to cover more of it, modular change offers specific benefits to all of the business first, then proceeds to offer more benefits.

Adopting a modular and/or incremental approach is a means of reducing risk. However, there are costs. Thinking about how to break the change down into chunks will take management time. There may be delay in the delivery of the benefits, which may (depending on the change) mean a delay in reducing costs or improving revenue. However, this could be offset by the potential to deliver early benefits or 'quick wins'.

Quick wins

Where the change is spread over a long period, you should aim for the achievement of a succession of 'quick wins', rather than planning for all the benefits to appear at the finish. A 'quick win' is a highly visible, concrete, indisputable benefit that clearly contributes to the change effort.

The advantages of the 'quick win' strategy are:

- those involved in the change effort can be justifiably rewarded and motivated
- there are ongoing benefits that offset the costs of the change effort
- a succession of quick wins maintains momentum on the change effort
- feedback on achievements helps to keep the change on track
- demonstration of benefits helps to maintain the support of corporate management for the change effort
- delivery of benefits helps to overcome resistance to change.

There are parallels with a modular approach; those modules achieved early on in a modular change programme would be similar to 'quick wins'. If you decide on a modular approach, consider which modules might be most advantageous in cultural terms to tackle first, in the sense of generating interest, support or enthusiasm.

change for the better

Transition

Any change that is significant to the business is bound to affect its operation for a time. You will need to give thought to how things will work during this transitional period.

The transition period should be recognised as a distinct state of the business, different from both the current and planned future states. It may be necessary to make interim arrangements for the transition period, such as:

- temporary hierarchies, project teams, and management responsibilities
- external services, temporary staff or consultants
- specific policies and procedures applying only to the transition period.

If you opt for transformational change, transition will be brief and probably highly disruptive in terms of business operation – possibly to the extent that no work is possible during the period. An example would be the replacement or installation of a new physical IT network in a business already reliant on such a network. The business would not be able to function as normal during transition.

If you opt for modular change, the transition period will be longer and punctuated by the advent of

the transition period is likely to be a time of stress and uncertainty

the benefits for each module. There will also be 'breathing spaces' after each module during which you can take stock and almost certainly learn some lessons from what has happened. Although there will be disruption, it will be localised, and there will only be interruptions to business operation where vital functions – or those through which all work must pass – are affected. Staff who are not yet affected by the change will be watching carefully; ensure that those who are affected have positive things to say about the change effort.

The situation will be similar in an incremental change process: a longer transition period, characterised by some local disruption but overall continuity. Lessons can be learned at any stage and aspects of the change transition 'tweaked' to smooth its progress.

As always, remember the importance of people issues. The transition period is likely to be a time of stress and uncertainty, and planning for the transition must take account of the concerns of those inside and outside the organisation who will be affected or who have a legitimate right to be kept informed. Keep the change moving, and ensure that the 'quick wins' it generates are visible and well known.

Unfreezing and refreezing

In order to ensure that the change will be accepted, and will endure, the change process must include the activities leading up to the change ('unfreezing'), and – just as important – the activities that follow up the change ('refreezing').

The 'unfreezing' phase is concerned with preparation for the change. The intention of this phase is to decrease people's commitment to the current procedures and make them aware of the need for the change, to counter resistance, and to generate support in favour of the change. Existing attitudes and beliefs are 'unfrozen' in preparation for the change, so that people will be receptive to it when it takes place.

Activities are likely to include:

- a programme of communication to ensure that all those concerned are kept fully informed
- involvement of staff in planning and preparation
- training and support for staff who will be affected by the change
- publicity campaigns to reinforce key messages about the change
- identifying and addressing resistance to the change.

change for the better

what will happen during the change?

The 'refreezing' phase, which follows the actual change, can be critical to its success – yet it is often neglected. Do not assume that the changes you make will be maintained as planned without positive action. The changes need to be institutionalised, and the business 'refrozen' in its new form. A key part of this is integrating the change into the culture of the business – not just creating a culture in which change is achievable, but also embedding the outcome of change into the business's culture, so that is becomes part of 'the way we do things'. Any or all of these tactics may be useful:

- **leading from the front:** senior management showing that they have embraced the change and are supporting it

- **monitoring** to ensure that the changes have taken place as planned and are being maintained

- **following up on new procedures** to ensure that they are being followed correctly

- **continuing support** to staff as they become familiar with the changes, such as through helpdesks and training

- **reinforcing changed attitudes and behaviours**, for example through publicity and incentive mechanisms such as rewards for appropriate behaviour (these must be perceived as fair and equitable)

- **diffusing new learning and practices** from pilot programmes, or those areas affected first by incremental change, to generate enthusiasm based on knowledge and understanding

- **applying sanctions** to discourage inappropriate behaviours

- **changing language and terminology** to emphasise cultural change – for example, by asking staff to refer to 'customers' instead of 'users' of a service

- **ensuring that the change is assimilated** into the beliefs, preferences and values of the business

- **redeploying or removing staff** who are particularly resistant to change or who are being obstructive to the change effort

- **recruiting staff** who are expected to be sympathetic to the change and are able to contribute positively

- **continuing positive efforts** to eliminate pre-change behaviours.

This perspective can be related to the force field analysis technique described in chapter 2. In the 'unfreezing' phase, the existing structure of forces is disturbed, and in the 'refreezing' phase a new configuration of forces, supportive of the new situation, is put in place and maintained. Part of the 'refreezing' task is to ensure that the old restraining forces do not return.

Remember that the business needs to keep running while it is being unfrozen and refrozen. You will almost certainly need additional resources during the transitional period to ensure this.

change for the better

6

people and change

this chapter is about the people involved in change: the people managing change, the people making it happen, and the people affected. People issues are often neglected in change management, but they have the power to make or break a programme of change.

The change owner

If nobody is responsible for a change, it is unlikely to succeed. Although this sounds obvious, many proposed changes founder for want of someone to take ownership and make them happen, and are destined instead to be batted around the meeting table indefinitely, even after they have become urgent. It is therefore crucial to identify the single individual who will be recognised throughout the business as the owner of the change and responsible for its success – the change owner.

The change owner's responsibilities in managing change are to plan the change, obtain approval for the change and its costs, obtain the resources required and ensure that everyone plays their part. Change owners provide a point of unitary authority with which the change can be identified. This can avoid the problems that characterise committee-run projects. Authority is much more effective when it rests, and is seen to rest, with a single individual.

However, this should not be seen as giving the change owner absolute power to drive through change against the will of others. A vital part of their role will be to ensure, and demonstrate, that the views of all stakeholders have genuinely been taken into account. The change owner needs to be a politician as well as a tactician. They will need credibility and diplomacy to deal with the cultural and human side of business change.

The change owner also ensures that the change process stays on track: that it delivers the benefits that were hoped for and does not lose focus or drift off target. One crucial authority held by the change owner is veto: the power to abandon the change if necessary.

For large-scale change, the change owner will need to be supported by a change team, with the skills to make change happen. See chapter 7 for more details.

change for the better

The importance of management commitment

Without the commitment and direct involvement of senior management, change is unlikely to progress very far. Senior management are responsible for defining the direction of the business. They must make clear their support for the change – if people affected by the change see a lack of commitment on their part, credibility will be damaged. Key managers should be seen to be taking a personal interest in the progress and achievements of the change effort.

Management must take the lead in establishing the values and behaviours required by the change effort, and this may mean leading by example. A good illustration is beginning to use new technology – if management do not use it, staff will not feel that they should have to.

Change champions

The commitment of management to the change effort is essential, but it is not sufficient to ensure success. As discussed in chapter 4, there will inevitably be a range of views on the proposed change. It is worth identifying 'change champions': individuals who support the change and who are in a position to influence others.

make time for change

A change champion is not necessarily a manager, or even a member of staff, but they do have power within the business. It may come from their expertise, their ability to influence colleagues, their network of contacts, or their understanding of politics and personalities. Change champions can become the public face of the change. They will make good members of task forces and focus groups. They will be well placed to generate ideas supporting the change, promote enthusiasm, communicate messages, and provide feedback on grass-roots reaction.

It will be easier to find change champions if they are, or can become, key stakeholders in the success of the change. While support is welcome from any quarter, a powerful ally who has much to gain from the success of the change will be invaluable.

Making time for change

Change means taking proactive steps to shape the business's destiny. Actions have to be justified in terms of long-term benefit rather than as responses to factors in the business environment. There is much more at stake – both financially and in reputational terms – than in times of 'business as usual'.

Even so, there is still a real danger that 'business as usual' activity –

change for the better

responding to the day-to-day demands of the business – can distract from the task of managing change. Dealing with issues that crop up can seem to be the most important task for management, but taking the line 'I must deal with this first – change can wait' is a dangerous game. It can result in years going by during which you are always 'too busy doing' to find time for change – although in retrospect, the problems that seemed urgent at the time could perhaps have been left, or delegated. Are you avoiding the larger issues by concentrating on smaller ones? Take a realistic look at the way your time has been allocated recently and ask yourself whether you will ever truly emerge from the woods of day-to-day pressures. Then bite the bullet and make time to look at what needs to change – today.

Communication

Successful change depends on communication. Amid the fear, uncertainty and doubt engendered by a major change, there is scope for rumour, half-truths and untruths to flourish. Those closest to the change process must take the lead in communicating information on the change – what will happen, what is happening, and what has happened – and the implications for all concerned.

The aims of the communication effort will be to:

- identify everyone who needs to be know about the change
- decide what are the key messages to get across (these should include the reasons for the change, its objectives, the benefits expected, and the approach that will be taken)
- decide which communication methods and media are most appropriate and cost-effective (face-to-face, written word, printed material, email, intranet/web, etc)
- decide how often, and in what length and format, interested parties should receive their communications
- make provision for two-way communication and feedback
- identify the communication responsibilities of the change owner, change team, management, change champions and others.

An important element will be a means of advertising success: disseminating information on 'quick wins'. Creating an atmosphere of progress and positive development will help to reduce resistance and combat cynicism.

successful change depends on communication

It will be vital for the communications to be co-ordinated with the other activities in the change effort – the message must be consistent with the action. If there are conflicts between the messages being issued and evidence on the ground, the credibility of the change effort will be undermined. Communications must be timely, honest, relevant and trustworthy. Information must also be complete; you can be sure that any gaps in coverage will be filled by corporate rumours.

Involvement and feedback

Involving people should be a part of the change effort from the start. Although it is beneficial to let people know what is planned, it is too late to inform them when concrete plans have already been made; this will imply that only their compliance, rather than their opinion, is relevant.

People will be more likely to accept the change if they have been involved in the planning and implementation processes. There must be opportunities to get staff involved in the decision-making; solicit opinions and ideas about problems or approaches. A suggested target is to get at least ten per cent of the affected workforce directly involved in decision-making for the change effort.

change for the better

People who have contributed their views in a constructive setting are more likely to endorse the rationale for the change. They must be encouraged to take ownership of the change and become committed to it. Taking account of different views demonstrates flexibility; it also allows the change owner to identify objections and deal with them.

Getting really useful feedback may require a cultural shift towards openness. People may be very unfamiliar or uneasy with direct, two-way communication at work; indeed, many may never have experienced it. They will need to feel confident that their input will be valued and taken on board. If management pay lip service to 'listening' and then drive through what was originally envisaged anyway, staff will be demoralised. Do not seek feedback on issues that you cannot control, or that it is too late to control. People will sense the emptiness of the gesture. You will not always be able to respond constructively to all feedback – indeed, you may hear some contradicting opinions. If you are not in a position to respond to a suggestion, say so – and explain why. Don't promise to respond at an unspecified time in the future if you know you will not be in a position to do so; you are merely storing up resentment for later.

If you feel that those giving feedback have not understood the aims of the change, look again at your communications plan. Have the aims of the change been clear from the start – to yourself, as well as others? Have they evolved? If people disagree with the way change is to be approached, ensure they have the big picture. It can be easy for those with a 'helicopter view' to assume that everyone knows everything that happens in the business, but this is not always so.

Do not make the mistake of trying to convince those who clearly stand to lose from change that they suffer for the greater good. It is no consolation that the business will be stronger if your role in it has been reduced (or removed). Straightforward honesty is the best policy.

People may worry that speaking out may be held against them in some way; to hear the most honest feedback you will need to instil in them the confidence that this will not happen. This feeling may be intensified if, for whatever reason, you are not in a position to respond to the concerns raised, staff may then feel they have said things that management did not want to hear. Explanations, coupled with reassurances that their feedback was valued, will help. In this (and in all communications), remember that it is human nature to assume the worst when nothing is heard from those in authority.

Training

When moving to new ways of working, everyone involved must be adequately prepared and supported. Training and development must be:

- tailored to the specific tasks of each individual or group
- reinforced with support facilities, counselling, refresher training and updates
- timed to match the timetable for change – training delivered too early will be forgotten, and therefore wasted
- repeated as necessary for new staff and those transferred to different duties.

Staff need to feel comfortable with the changes, and feel confident in their abilities to work in new ways; otherwise they may revert to old habits and modes of operation. Plans must be made for support facilities such as helpdesks, support groups, documentation and online help facilities, and liaison officers to support individual workgroups. The staff who will need most help should be identified and special arrangements made for them.

Training and personal development need to go beyond the transfer of the mechanical skills required for new systems or procedures. It also presents an opportunity to change the culture of the business. Attitudes and behaviours are closely linked, and you will need to consider where to concentrate your efforts – will new ways of working help to generate new attitudes, or will changing people's attitudes help to embed new ways of working?

The first weeks or months following a change will be critical for those affected, and it is essential to provide support facilities to deal with queries, problems and suggestions. People must not feel that they have been left to 'sink or swim' with the new arrangements, and allowance must be made for those who have genuine difficulty in adapting. Having said that, it must also be made clear that returning to old ways is not an option.

For example, conformance with the new arrangements can be publicly recognised or rewarded, and failure to demonstrate the required change challenged. If it seems that lack of conformance with the new arrangements goes unnoticed, then people will naturally come to believe that management are not serious about the change, and 'backsliding' will occur.

An emphasis on staff training and development may itself represent a culture change for the business – but it is an essential element in successful change.

Overcoming resistance to change

People are remarkably adaptable, but they will resist change if they think it will leave them worse off. They are bound to ask what the change will mean for them personally, and arguments based on 'the good of the business' will carry less weight than personal considerations. If people broadly accept the way things are, they are likely to see the disadvantages of any change before they acknowledge the (perhaps less obvious) advantages.

Resistance to change may arise from:

- **fear of the unknown:** people will resist change if they feel it is a 'leap in the dark'
- **fear of failure:** people may be uncertain of their ability to handle new tasks or technology
- **concern over changes to established practice:** people may worry that the change will overturn the traditions of the business
- **lack of confidence in management:** people may not believe that the change is adequately managed; or that there is too much reliance on external support (such as management consultants)
- **lack of involvement** in planning or managing change
- **misunderstandings:** people may simply have the wrong idea about what is intended
- **power changes:** change is likely to be interpreted in terms of winners and losers; those who think they will lose will oppose it
- **personal changes:** to working or employment conditions, remuneration, or perceived standing within the business
- **corporate memory:** previous attempts at changing the business will influence people's attitudes now.

The list could go on and on; there are many possible sources of resistance to change, and a critical task will be to identify and anticipate resistance, and take steps to address it. Force field analysis, as described in chapter 2, may help to identify the forces acting against change, and focus thought on the best way to overcome or reduce them.

There are many ways to deal with resistance. The importance of communication and involving staff in decision-making has already been covered. Other approaches include:

- **make trade-offs:** grant something of value in exchange for less resistance and more commitment to the change

- **work through 'change champions':** use the power relationships and groupings within the business to favour the change. Ensure the change is sponsored by managers with high charisma, prestige and influence – coupled with legitimate power

- **create group prestige:** make it attractive and desirable to be 'on side', pushing change forward

- **give special consideration to staff who can obstruct the change:** for example, by offering them key roles in the change team or a stake in decision-making

- **retain links with the past:** don't assume that people will welcome the announcement of 'improvements'. Criticism of past situations may be taken as criticism of the individuals who helped to create them, or failed to change them. Perhaps present change as 'supporting' or 'building on' current operations rather than 'replacing' or 'improving' them

- **retain familiar practices:** do not change things arbitrarily; retain established workgroups and routines where possible, to reduce the impact of the change (but not where they would inhibit the change). Changes embedded in the immediate work situation tend to be more lasting

- **form coalitions:** work to establish agreements among those with common goals, where their combined strength and commitment will help the change

- **demonstrate the drivers for change:** involve resistant staff in the collection, consideration and analysis of information that supports or suggests change.

change for the better

people will resist
change if they
think it will leave
them worse off

Pilots and demonstrations

Where there are doubts about the feasibility of the change proposal, a pilot project can be a good way to investigate the issues and risks further. Ideally, the pilot would be conducted in a controlled environment, isolated from the rest of the business's normal operations, to give a clear picture of its workings. An example would be constructing a mock-up of new workplace arrangements to test new procedures or IT systems.

Pilots should be on a scale that is economical for the business to handle, but at the same time they must be large enough to accurately mimic the proposed change.

The pilot will enable the change team to assess what will and will not work in the future, and the advantages and disadvantages of different approaches. It may also cast doubts on the viability of the change as a whole. Assuming this does not happen and the change proceeds, whatever you find out from the pilot can help to reduce the risks before going any further.

It may be appropriate to use external experts or assessors in pilot projects to enhance the credibility of the results.

A demonstration project may help to persuade doubters of the desirability of the proposed change, that it will work and will be acceptable. The demonstration project should replicate the conditions expected 'in the real world' as far as possible.

In a situation where you are facing both technical difficulties and resistance to change, the approach might be to implement a pilot project to iron out the technical problems, followed by a demonstration project to win over the doubters.

change for the better

7

roles

- The change owner
- Senior management
- The change team

his chapter outlines the responsibilities for the major roles in change, together with a summary of the skills and experience that those who fill them will need.

Some team roles may require full-time staffing throughout the change; others may require part-time or fluctuating coverage. Invariably, the change team will combine people who are working full-time on the change with others who divide their time between the change effort and other duties.

The stakeholders in a change also have parts to play. As a group they will be varied, ranging from those who are expected to play an active part in making the change happen to those whose roles are largely passive but whose commitment is still important because of the power they have to impede or resist the change. Some stakeholders are bodies or organisations; others are individuals.

The change owner

Overall responsibility, leadership and authority for the change is assigned to the role of change owner.

The appointed change owner may only be involved part-time, but they must be visibly and consistently the driving force. The change owner is ultimately accountable for the success of the change and the individual appointed must have authority to direct it effectively.

The change owner has personal accountability for realising the benefits and is responsible for:

- 'owning' the vision for the change
- overall control of implementation, with personal responsibility for achieving the change (this should be an important measure of their individual performance)
- securing the investment required to make change happen and realise the benefits
- establishing the change initiative, securing sufficient team resources and monitoring progress
- managing communication with stakeholders
- ensuring that the business and staff are managed carefully through the process of change

change for the better

- ensuring that the aims of the change stay aligned with evolving business needs
- commissioning reviews that formally assess the results of change and the benefits realised.

Senior management

The role of senior management as a key stakeholder group is to ensure that the change contributes to business strategy. They must be committed to the change and maintain that commitment throughout the life of the change. They must lead by example and proactively foster enthusiasm for the change.

choose the right people to make change happen

The change team

Larger changes will almost certainly need a dedicated team, reporting to the change owner, to make them happen. The people involved will need a range of skills, both technical and cultural.

Technical skills might include:

- knowledge of the business
- project management
- risk management
- problem solving and conflict/dispute resolution
- business process analysis and re-engineering
- skills in collecting and interpreting information
- understanding of relevant IT issues.

On the cultural side, the 'people skills' required will include:

- communication and persuasion
- diplomacy and tact
- a grasp of the concept of 'culture' in business, and a conscious understanding of the culture of your particular business
- the ability and willingness to listen
- understanding of the views of stakeholders, and ideally a personal acquaintance with some or all of the individuals involved.

If the change team is to achieve success, it must include innovators and creative thinkers. Staff who are wedded to the status quo are unlikely to generate the momentum required for pushing through the change. A balance needs to be struck between new and respected faces, as well as between experience, enthusiasm and expertise.

The change team has to have credibility, or it will struggle for authority. The team members must be respected by management and staff for their sensitivity to the concerns of all stakeholders, while retaining the authority to drive through change.

The physical location of the team can be important. If the team is located remotely from the rest of the business, there is a danger that it may be regarded as isolated, out of touch and therefore irrelevant.

change for the better

8

after the change

- Realising the benefits
- Knock-on effects
- Reward and celebrate success

Once the change is over, you need to make sure that the benefits you hoped for have been realised. You also need to look at what effects change has had, and whether they suggest more changes. Last but not least, take time to celebrate successful change.

Realising the benefits

Before a change, you need to identify the benefits that will be obtained when your objectives have been achieved. Each benefit needs to be expressed in terms of where it will occur, who will benefit, who is responsible for its delivery, and how it will be measured. Once change is over, you need to check that each benefit you hoped for has actually been realised.

Documenting the desired benefits at an early stage will help to keep efforts focused on the real aims of change. It is important to remember that not all benefits are desirable, even though they may be positive for the business. As the change progresses, it may transpire that other benefits could be realised. But they could end up distracting you from your key objectives – particularly if they are easy to achieve in comparison with them. There is a danger of focusing on simple, short-term or purely financial benefit at the expense of complex, long-term benefits for the whole business. Benefits management throughout change helps you focus on what you should do, rather than what you could do.

Benefits can be realised in areas such as improved efficiency, financial saving, reduced risk, improved service to customers, and better internal management. Others will be 'soft' benefits – the public image of the business, for example, or a more motivated workforce.
It is important to recognise the importance of these soft benefits, even though they may be harder to quantify.

Knowing what benefits will result from change forms a key part of the cultural side of change, since people will want to know 'what's in it for them'. Communicating the benefits that will result from change can be vital to overcoming resistance. Soft benefits are vital – benefits need to be expressed in human terms as well as in terms of efficiency or profit. Soft benefits must also be concrete improvements that can be shown to have worked, not empty promises used to convince doubters or drive change through against people's wishes.

not all benefits
are financial

Some benefits depend on other benefits for their realisation. Benefits that make other benefits possible are known as enabling benefits, or lower-order benefits. Benefits that come about as a result of realising these benefits are known as higher-order benefits. It may be that only the higher-order benefits are part of your strategy for the business. Understanding the structure and interdependencies of benefits is vital in large-scale change.

learn from the impacts of the change

It is also important to consider the 'dis-benefits' from change. Dis-benefits are unfavourable outcomes of change; you may or may not have anticipated them before you began, but it is important to take them all into account when reviewing the change. It may be that dis-benefits suggest new change projects.

Knock-on effects

Once the implications of the original change have worked themselves through, the need for further changes often becomes clear. Such knock-on effects may arise because the change worked out differently from expected, or because the desired change was not achieved, or simply because there are unforeseen consequences of the change – not necessarily negative.

Even where the desired changes are achieved successfully, there may be knock-on effects that can prevent the business from 'refreezing' in its new form. For example, the introduction of a new IT system may appear to realise benefits of increased efficiency, but there may be other consequences on a human level, affecting job security, career opportunities, stress, and individuals' status and autonomy.

Knock-on effects will affect your ability to realise benefits fully. Obviously, the future is always unclear, but you should consider what might happen as far as possible when planning for change:

- be prepared for a continuous process of change and development as the the effects of change ripple through the business
- be prepared to recognise unintended consequences of change, including benefits that were not originally planned
- be prepared for experimentation and backtracking
- learn from the impacts of the change, and feed this learning forward to subsequent change efforts
- recognise that no design for change can be complete
- recognise that if people think something is going to change, they may act accordingly even if no change is actually planned; perceived change can be as influential as real change.

Reward and celebrate success

When the change is complete and new ways of working have 'taken root', remember to reward those who have contributed to the success of the change. This includes those to whom promises were made, but also anyone who made a difference. With the change team, and anyone else who has got involved, take time to celebrate success and state out loud how well the process has gone. This binds the change team together and demonstrates to everyone that their efforts are productive, beneficial and appreciated by management. It also reinforces the principle that success depends on collective effort.

Communication should not stop at the end of the change, and an important part of it is to thank those who have helped with the change. It is also useful to let people know how the benefits of the change are helping the business to grow and develop, and how this might translate into personal benefit for those who embraced change. When those who were implacably resistant to change see the rewards and benefits of success, they may get more involved next time.

Rewarding and celebrating success is important in laying the foundations for further changes. People do not want to feel that their efforts were taken for granted, and may not be so keen to help next time if their contributions are accepted without acknowledgement. Keep in mind what things were like before, how far you have come since then and the sacrifices that people have made along the way.

change for the better

Index